DES DILLO... award-winning writer. Also a stand up comic, his novel *Me and Ma Gal* was shortlisted for the Saltire Society First Book of the Year Award and won the World Book Day 'We Are What We Read' poll for the novel that best describes Scotland today and was selected as one of *The List* / Scottish Book Trust's 100 All Time Best Scottish Books. His poetry and short stories have been anthologised internationally. His latest award was The Lion and Unicorn prize for the best of Irish and British literature in the Russian Language (2007). The Russian language version of his hit play *Six Black Candles* has been running in Kiev since March 2010 and a production by Goldfish Theatre – founded by Des in 2010 – recently undertook an extensive tour of Scotland. He is the writer of the smash hit phenomenon of Scottish culture, *Singin I'm No a Billy He's a Tim*, probably the most-performed play in Scotland in the last five years. Des lives in Galloway.

Also by Des Dillon:

FICTION

Me and Ma Gal (1995)
The Big Empty: A Collection of Short Stories
  (1996)
Duck (1998)
Itchycooblue (1999)
Return of the Busby Babes (2000)
Six Black Candles (2002)
The Blue Hen (2004)
The Glasgow Dragon (2004)
Singin I'm No A Billy He's A Tim (2006)
They Scream When You Kill Them (2006)
Monks (2007)
My Epileptic Lurcher (2009)
An Experiment in Compassion (2011)

POETRY

Picking Brambles (2003)

SCUNNERED

Slices of Scottish life
in seventeen gallus syllables

BY

DES DILLON

LUATH PRESS

EDINBURGH

First published 2011

ISBN : 978-1-908373-01-4

The publisher acknowledges subsidy from

towards the publication of this book

The paper used in this book promotes sustainable forest
management and is PEFC credited material.

Printed and bound by
Martins the Printers, Berwick Upon Tweed

Typeset in 12 point Sabon by
3btype.com

Do I contradict myself?
Very well, then I contradict myself,
I am large, I contain multitudes.

WALT WHITMAN

CONTENTS

[7]

PREFACE

I didn't set out here to write esoteric poems. But everyone will find some of these poems impenetrable. That's because we've read different books.

Even how I set these poems on the page affects them, or even infects them, or even, when the meaning is powerfully changed – effects them. It's a bit like quantum theory – the observer having an influence on the experiment – these haikus have an influence on each other to a greater or lesser extent. Pure meaning is impossible unless each poem is published on its own piece of clean white paper. And there is no such a thing as clean white paper.

Another thing has happened – the haiku can force the reader to leap between the second line and the last line and make a sense not explicit in the poem. This phenomenon has spread into the collection so that narratives start to appear between poems. It seems narrative sits spring loaded behind all juxtaposition.

DES DILLON

[SCIENCE AND NATURE]

ARROGANCE

Go to the mirror.
Say – I may be gravely wrong
and you may be right.

UNIVERSITY

What we know has been
limited by the closed
down questions we ask.

APOCALYPSE

We must realise
we deal with tiny numbers
still too big to count.

A HISTORY OF INSTRUMENTATION

We are obsessed
by precision yet cannot
measure our own lives.

A WAY FORWARD

Between abstract and
empiricism we find
Newton's beaming smile.

FRANCIS BACON

Things never done can
only be done in a way
never before tried.

DARWIN'S PETIT EVOLUTION

There's no designer
in evolution. But what
of clear light of love?

DARWIN'S PARADOX

Yet we cannot bring
about any new species
with all of Science.

EINSTEIN'S RUSH

What's empirical
about riding the edge of
a white beam of light?

FORCE EQUALS MASS TIMES SOMETHING ELSE

If there was no Earth
where would this stone come
    to rest?
Gravity's centre?

HEY! WE'RE GOING THE
WRONG WAY

Now we can think of
survival of the fittest
in the wrong shaped hole.

NOBODY KNOWS NOTHING

I am just like you –
Regarding the Universe:
I only work here.

SUCCULENCE

Did you ever think
a peach the womb of the tree
where the seed shall grow?

HOLY VERTIGO

It was the trembling
heart of magnificence this
drop through snow and sun.

MESOLITHIC

Among springtime stones
a wind brings the same old scents
over tests of time.

WHITE RAIN

A wood pigeon flaps
cracking springtime twigs.
Petals on my head.

BEARING THE CROWN

Red like heat, yet cold,
your berries are lips. Unborn,
springtime lies like iron.

GLENCOE

A rush to see you.
Sheets of cloud shadow moving
over white mountains.

SUMMIT

Yes, I see beauty
and I tremble – again – I'm
face to face with death.

DARK

When the day is done
we turn away from the sun
and face cold cold space.

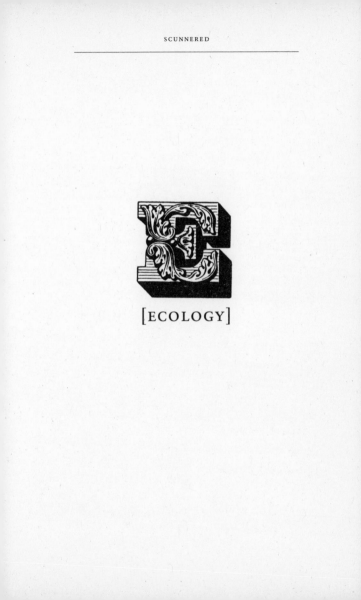

[ECOLOGY]

ENCROACH

Villages, towns and
cities are machines in the
war against nature.

THE TRAVELLER

Wanted church. But found
a glowing petrol station
through spindles of trees.

REDRAFT

With roads and smog and
bombs and natural aplomb,
we edit God's work.

US

The most successful
predators on the planet.
The most unnatural.

STOIC NONSENSE ON STILTS

Animals have no
language and so can't reason
therefore feel no pain.

ISOLATION

We'll never decode
the language of animals,
that one true Babel.

POWER WITHOUT MANDATE

If the animals
had the weapons, I know who
they'd be coming for.

CULPABILITY

Trying to reach calves
cows crash into barbed wire.
And me? I drink milk.

BEND

Can't get up. The wings
flapping for each ounce of life.
These just hit ducklings.

SWERVING

Saw the pink minced guts
of an M8 deer. Thank fuck!
Just a dead carpet.

A701

A stoat ran across,
same one same place as last time.
Does that mean something?

CYCLICAL

Comes the fire that burns,
the fire that burns winds and
   snows
making again: ice.

CONSUMERISM

The weight, and the weight
and the rising tide, that is
the burden of stuff.

CARBON REFUGEES

Two hundred million people
makes the potato famine
look like a picnic.

MORNING HAS BROKEN

The world is reborn.
Grass is sacred. Floating cows
mooove on hover-hooves.

WIND TURBINES

I pray one day that
they will turn and torque the
    earth
new through winds of change.

MESSAGE FROM THE WORLD

My children, were you
dead I'd love you unaware
you didn't want me.

EARTHMESSAGE

My tears are petrol;
breath – smoky. My heart
　　is black
grieving you, not me.

[FAMILY]

NUCLEAR FAMILY

We stand together
staring at mutually
assured destruction.

SEE

Ordinary folk
on investigation are
extraordinary.

MOTHER'S ADVICE

You need money to
be able to believe that
you don't need money.

FATHER'S ADVICE

Don't buy what you can
steal and don't steal what you can
pick up for nothing.

SAWMILL

The scent of new wood
reminds me of my father.
The sting of his fists.

ORPHAN

The smell of chip fat
reminds me of my mother
being drunk that day.

MY SON'S TROUBLES

Sins of the father
will be visited upon
the son, by the son.

HOMELESS FATHER

This city's winter
morning's moon-dark gauze.
You, out there somewhere.

AFTER THE CAR CRASH

They're looking old now.
Maybe a chunk of life-force
shears off on impact.

RESTITUTION

Getting older starts
the burgers you bought your weans
coming back at you.

GUILT

My brother winked
as he entered the high dock.
His sentence? Ten years.

BLIND MAN'S BLUFF

Me? Humility?
Noted for humility
me, noted for it.

STALLED

I said to Jim – do
you know who I think I am?
His fist stopped short.

COFFIN

I remember Jim
moving our granddad's dead hands.
Now these are his hands.

SAVING CLICHÉ

Beneath that hard hard
exterior there preys a
cruel interior.

SCHOOL PHOTOS

Some were wimpy, some
bossy. Others risen to
high scorn and envy.

[SCOTLAND AND POLITICS]

SUPERIORITY

A small country where
snobbery is mistaken
for morality.

SCOTLAND

They played their hearts out.
Oh man you should have seen them.
Aw! The way We lost.

SCOTTISH HAIKU

Edinburgh and
Glasgow – separated by
a common language.

POSITIVE THINKING

Nobody's ever
more than two metres from a rat.
Nor from a poem.

SCOTTISH VILLAGE

You'll be accepted
when they feel they know you well
enough to hate you.

STRANGERS

Superstition comes
with them and their open arms
fill our hearts with dread.

FUEL

At the least wee thing
we turn the hate up full blast.
We'll never break free.

THE WALL

I've noticed, in schools,
this aspiration vacuum;
a resignation.

OSCAR WILDE'S SCOTLAND

All in the gutter.
It's just that some are looking
down on the others.

NEDS

Suck gift on gift in
no matter how great. Black holes
where we want mirrors.

ARISTOTLE ON SCOTLAND

Nature produces
nothing without good reason;
save midges and neds.

DISSOLUTION

Neds marking our streets.
Fear reigns. It is far far deep
Thatcher resonates.

PANDORA'S BOX

Thatcher opened it.
This nation devoured it.
Greed, hate, rage, lust: all.

PANDORA'S OTHER BOX

Thatcherism and
all these years of me me me
equals guns and knives.

VITAPHOBIC

Gorge on drink and drugs;
bigging up oblivion.
Terrified of life.

AMERICAN DREAM

You say go for it,
we say don't make waves, so let's
call the whole thing off.

SCOTTISH WILL TO POWER

Pontificating;
eloquent, passionate. But:
procrastination.

EMIGRANT ÉMIGRÉ

I have been too much
in lands other than my own.
I have become strange.

SCOTLENGLAND

No armies here nor
bombs nor guns. But laws and lies
still colonise us.

SCOTSOPHRENIA

Caledonian
antisyzygy; here still.
Sunday Post and *Mail*.

NATIONALIST

Standing with the flag,
he's some kind of Superman.
Tell that to Hitler.

EXPLOILTED

Tell me – where is my
hundred and seventy grand
from all of Our oil?

THE LONG DEBATE

The East and the West,
never the twain shall meet till
the last word is in.

OIL

So we go to war
this day on a collective
misunderstanding.

IMPEDIMENT

War can never end.
We'll never wind down to peace
because we are want.

BLAME GAME

They're easy targets
for poets and terrorists,
these Americans.

IRISH IMMIGRANT

Was just new after
praying for you so I was.
And now you're here too.

SUBJECT

He's coming in at
ten o clock and he'll kill you
so he will my Da.

BLOKADA

Leningrad City
Executive Committee,
where's our daily bread?

CULTURAL RELATIVISM

They love their engines
the same way we love our dogs.
This is Africa.

[THE ARTS]

SHAVED HEAD

You don't understand
because you are fuckin thick.
That's the art we like.

BLACK POLO NECK

You don't understand
cos I'm a fuckin genius.
That's the art we like.

SCOTTISH ARTS I

Nice London lassies,
dangerous with good degrees;
giving me advice.

THESE WHO TEACH

Why are PhD's
not out there writing *King Lear*?
Huckleberry Finn.

SCOTTISH ARTS 2

I have been shaved
like a witch by your insults.
And no mark was found.

CRITICISM

You cannot reject
me until you accept me.
That's where this must start.

BABY ETHICS

The measure of all
things. It used to be man but
now it's the BBC.

FILM AND TELLY

Mac6hia6vel6lian
with five extra vowels and
three silent numbers.

HISTORY OF THE ENGLISH LANGUAGE

Bucket or pail or
quisling or quail that's how
we know who you are.

SNOBBERY

Intelligence fell
like snow you know, not only
among posh voices.

ON WRITING HAIKU

Always remember
Sidney and Spencer
John Milton, Dryden and Pope.

SS

The short sentence is
the beautiful sentence. Short
sentence. Sentence. Short.

SAME DIFFERENCE

You say bloody thing.
I say fuckin thing, so let's
call the whole thing off.

SINE NOBILITATE

The distance from the
glottal stop to the alveolar?
Infinite judgement.

DEEP POWER

In my life's struggles
I have enlisted language
in many guises.

NOAM CHOMSKY

Under changing seas
language shoals and sometimes
    leaps.
I windsurf above.

DECAY

Would I rather me
or my work be eternal?
That is a hard one.

THE BALANCE

Every creative
act has to bring about death.
Even this poem.

BARBARIANS

The Bible's power;
ancient acts reminding us
we have not changed.

ROMEO! JULIET!

They call when falling
in love. And as a warning.
In desolation.

MEDEA AND THE DRINK

I'm smashing the house
and telling myself to stop:
this point of reason.

THE GREAT GATSBY

The flip-side of the
American dream is the
ghostly nobody.

POETRY IS

Drawing a circle.
It's in there somewhere but you
can't quite get to it.

POETRY

Is trying to make
inadequate language strike
where arrows can't stick.

THE SKIMMING

It's a nervous age
and we can't break the surface
of artistic light.

ORIGINALITY?

One shoal's direction
turns on a flash of light – now –
same shoal: no one fish.

FIVE SEVEN FIVE

To get seventeen
syllables you have to be
manipulative.

MONOSYLLABIC

If it is, it is.
So it is so; so it is.
It is as it is.

BIRTH

In the beginning
was the word and the word was
fuck; language begins.

1786

Racoon enters the
English language like a wee
Indian rocket.

TRANSCENDING SCOTLAND

While I am bursting out –
if I should break anything –
let it be your glass.

MAVERICK

They're planning there still
and drinking. But I furrowed
my own revolution.

PARADISE LUST

Wow! Across the class
her Paradise-Lost held tight
between silky legs.

LOWRY

Leaving factories
crouched over in snow; faces
lit by mobile phones.

[PSYCHOLOGY]

THE NECESSARY BLINKERS

Life – a series of
disappointments glued brightly
together by hope.

DENIAL

Most plums think that they'll
never be prunes, but all plums
are prunes in the end.

ATTENTION SEEKERS

Self-assertion is
the very heart and core of
all conversation.

SELECTIVE PERCEPTION

We're not tuned in,
for we pick up everything
while we know nothing.

WHAT THOUGHT SAYS

The mind is a good
servant but a bad master.
Think me, I am real.

CONSTRUCTION

Concrete is a good
servant but a bad master.
My thoughts are my cell.

COURAGE

You can take a thought
to the edge of a high cliff
but can't make it leap.

THE PATH

You must realise
you are in your own prison.
Then you can break free.

FLOWERHEAD

People wear culture
like a uniform so that
we see who they are.

TASTE

His caricature
is another man's fetish.
The extremes of same.

RACE?

It's the beginning
of your journey forward this
day; do not compare.

POV

William wanted the
next chapter but his dog it
wanted a thrown stick.

ATTITUDE

Treating every time
like it's the very last time
feels like the first time.

SUPPORT

Do not let words of
support stray into advice.
This is not friendship.

ASYLUM

Dancing to music –
Steve Wright in the afternoon
from my prison cell.

EGGSHELL

Through the weaknesses
in walls we put up, the past
rips into present.

GALE FORCE THINKING

It's windy today
and bringing up great ocean
    waves.
I'm still lost at sea.

ALCOHOL

Exploding in the
timeline of my life. So take
a look at me now.

HOPE

Watching a house dark
on a hill through creaking trees.
Then; one candle lights.

LEAP OF FAITH

I will live my life
no more in the belief that
something will turn up.

NO FEAR MY ARSE

I windsurf and rock
climb and kayak down rivers
cos fear is my fuel.

THE VEILS

I don't want to die
on the dawning of knowledge
that I did not live.

P

[PHILOSOPHY]

WE ARE

Babylonian
and the Dionysian –
all things in between.

UPANISHAD

Sitting next to the
master and learning what you
say to the master.

ADRIANNE'S THREAD

The semaphoric
dance of the returning bee
maps out sweet flowers.

DIGITIZING HISTORY

Dance, Song, then Drama,
held Truth. Now all's recorded.
Nothing is chosen.

HERODOTUS NOT FREUD

Men, moved by symbols,
or words, at war, do not hate.
They fight for their cause.

SPOTS AND PLOOKS

My granny wasn't
Hippocrates. She saw the
badness seep out me.

BUMPKIN PHILOSOPHERS

Common sense isn't
that common because no-one
seems to possess it.

CAUSE AND EFFECT

Martians might assume
the indicator light moves
the car left and right.

ANTIGONE

We must have innate
laws – how could we generate
a society?

NO MORE HEROES

Can virtue be taught?
Bring back what are the Heroes
and watch what they do.

LEARNING PYTHAGORAS

What does not square is
that they never said he was
vegetarian.

MESSIAH

You, Aristotle,
were the Jesus of the mind.
You set out our course.

DEEP THOUGHT – OR CREATIVITY?

Okay folks, I want
you to name two Renaissance
philosophers. Eh?

SPARK

These bones and muscles
they are the amplifiers
of dendrites sparking.

PHENOMENALISM

Mind is gravity
drawing all these sensations
into blocks of real.

LEIBNIZ

The intellect lays
in wait for experience.
Ambushing a life.

SCHILLER'S DIVINITY

When we are at play
we are become God. And we
float in the spirit.

SEPARATE SOUL?

Are we products of
our bits, or sitting tenants
paying rent of pain.

EMPATHETIC

I'm a happy man
because I know why Nietzsche
hugged that sick horse.

WITTGENSTEIN'S FLY – AS FUCK

He grinned when he told
Russell he'd nothing to say –
left clutching the prize.

PARISTOTLEDOX

By his nature man
is a social animal
who wants left alone.

ARISTOTLE'S DEAD PENDULUM

If virtue is the
midpoint between two extremes
where's the bumps of life?

HEDONISM

Reason find me ways
to satisfy my passion
then back in your box.

TRIBAL

Not with anger nor
aggression do countries war
but with pure devotion.

A QUESTION OF KNOWLEDGE

Aristotle says –
all men desire by nature
to know... But I feel.

THE CITY OF GOD

Intuition, vast
and ranging over all fields,
versus proud reason.

SHACKLES

Orthodoxy has
been killing the long debate.
We must save its life.

FLORENTINE ARCHITECTURE

Does morality
imitate art, or does art
imitate morals?

IDEO-SECULAR RELIGION

It is not by fact
we live, but by our million
articles of faith.

SPECIES

Why did God create
his masterpiece Man so late?
Interest or debate?

RELEASE FROM TORPOR

We have to accept
there are certain mysteries
we can surf with faith.

TWICE CURSED

No wonder witches
float – osteoporosis
makes old ladies light.

DESCARTES

I think so I am.
But I am aware I think
so, I am, therefore.

CANYONS OF THE SOUL

Sits a great chasm
between mind and body and
everyday – we leap.

LAW

In different clothes
we have different duties.
My wardrobe's too full.

OMEGA

The mind is furnished
by experience, but John,
where does that begin?

RESPONSIBILITY

How can I have this
personal identity
now I'm different cells?

MARRIAGE

I am the same man
but I'm not the same person.
Let's move together.

DON'T BE COMMITTED
TO HEMLOCK

I live each day at
one with my philosophy
changing all the time.

THESE ARE GOOD BISCUITS,
BUT

If I was exempt
from moral judgement, I would
kill for a biscuit.

KANT'S MORAL IMPERATIVE

We don't fall by chance,
freedom makes morality.
We fall down with wings.

HUME

Inside of us lives
a nub or morality
around which we grow.

CLINICAL

The Enlightenment
sold the antiques and furnished
with IKEA.

WHERE HAVE YOU GONE JOE
DIMAGGIO?

There is one thing that
explains Romanticism,
that thing is wonder.

IN THE KINGDOM OF FREEDOM

How do free beings
ever know that they are free?
All moves may be false.

NO MAHLER

If I gave you all
the pieces you'd never know
what radio is.

NIETZSCHE'S EROS

This statue here is
a concrete euphemism
for power and rape.

NIETZSCHE'S HINDRANCE

The body and the
senses stop the fool seeing
what is really true.

UTILITARIANISM

In our freedom we
have raped and killed and burned.
John Stuart Mill was wrong.

EVOLUTION OF CONSCIOUSNESS?

You can't be a wee
bit pregnant and you can't be
a wee bit conscious.

A NATION BUILT ON COAL

At night I dream of
Matthew's sweetness and his
  light –
juxtaposed with coal.

EGO – SUPER EGO

Even at death we're
never quite reconciled.
Inside – all's at war.

GANDHI

What do you think of
Western Civilisation?
We should try it out.

ELITE

Philosophy should
not be for the few, it should
lace our minds like dew.

THE GREAT MUST

We daily question
knowledge, truth and governance.
Sand grains: universe.

IN THE END WHAT ARE WE?

Flame on clay or brain
on mind hanging together.
No mortal will know.

[SPIRITUALITY]

THE BIG BLOOM

God is the Big Bang.
We are all things; his exploding
thoughts and all actions.

LISTS

Must do, have to do,
will one day sit in the breeze
of my final breath.

YOUR PATH

Those who imitate
great people absorb all things
save what makes them great.

WATCHING MEDITATION

My big dog Bailey
runs about mad in autumn:
catchy fally leafs.

ONLY THIS

Time past; memory.
Time future; expectation.
Time present: insight.

SAMSÃRA

We are all ghosts
living in haunted houses
we call our bodies.

DOWNWIND

I'm walking behind
my epileptic lurcher,
farting as he goes.

THOUGHT

Cumbersome and slow;
trees hold the insight to twist
their face to the light.

RAPTURE

People get ready,
lest we miss the great events
which sit by tea cups.

THE ROAD TO ENLIGHTENMENT

Sheets of milky rain
fill these gaps in summer pine.
There's no dry way home.

SPIRITUAL

One hour in darkness
is worth much much much
    more than
an hour in the light.

GOD

The things of the cosmos
are composed by the shockwaves
of your promises.

TRANSFIGURATION

No Devils. No Gods.
Jesus refusing to rise:
Galilee's Buddha.

DREAD

This breath is seamless
with future breath and I fear
I'm already dead.

PRAYER

The Gods are silent
and in dark shadows I stand
asking what am I.

INTIMATIONS OF MORTALITY

These days come in like
waves until my tide turns and
I'm drifting away.

RIPPLES

I slide one cold hand
into this still Solway Sea:
touching everything.

YIN AND YANG

Fishing; a merging
of quiet meditation
and the gambling buzz.

PANTHEISTIC

Do I hear thunnor?
Or the one true God rolling
two true wheely bins?

HA HA LLELUJAH

Cosmic but comic
angels fly because they take
being holy lightly.

ABUSE

To save us from hell
Jesus took a right beating
from his dear old dad.

REPRESSION

Eve bit the apple
so that we could really see
what life was about.

WHAT IS SIN?

The more we sin the
more mortal we become. It
all makes perfect sense.

FACELIFT

Transfiguration
in life – your face and wrinkles;
human yet Devine.

HAPPY

Guilty all my life
of wanting to be happy,
instead of being.

TO DIE

Surf or ski or leap
into your grave screaming joy.
That's the way to live.

THE HUMAN HIATUS

I have to tell you
this is not your beginning –
life started before.

THE BIG BREATH

The cosmos expands
and contracts. One of the great
lungs of the great God.

[LOVE]

TRUE COLOURS

I saw through your lines
like venetian blinds, to see
what lies within you.

FORLORN

I'm thinking of the
probability of love.
Supply and demand.

SEPARATION

When they are leaving
on a rainy winter day,
trains are like dying.

LONGING

Monday morning – wet.
Then, white in my wing mirror;
a rhododendron.

RECONCILIATION

To say I love you
and that your cold winter moon
is my summer moon.

HOW TO STAY FAITHFUL

People at home want
and need me. And that is a
good true clean feeling.

KAYAK DOG

Out round the blue buoy,
his arse snug in the spray deck.
Big paws on the bow.

MEETING YOU

I came to a stage
where I couldn't fall in love
with beauty alone.

GEOMETRY OF LUST

When I think of you
driving home on a dark night
I think curvy thoughts.

NO CONNECTION

But the bigger the
orgasm you have the more
flowers bloom in woods.

MATHEMATICS OF LOVE

My height divided
by your height is the
divine proportion.

MOURNING

Had I six months left,
I'd live again any six
spent with you alive.

ADDICTS

We are addicted
to our own Desires. We can
never love others.

LOVE

Has proved to be this:
finding you gradually
in sharp and blunt days.

GHOST

On our shoreline bench,
stumbled by my sudden smile,
I recognise you.

PERFECT MOMENT

The woman I love.
The vast and scattered cosmos
and silence. Silence.

An Experiment in Compassion

Des Dillon

ISBN 978 1906817 73 2 PBK £8.99

Stevie's just out of jail. Newly sober and building a relationship with his son, he's taking control of his own life. But what about his younger brother, Danny?

In this touching and darkly funny story of retribution and forgiveness, Stevie battles against the influences that broke him before, while Danny and his girlfriend spiral further into self-destruction. Can the bond between the two brothers be enough to give them both a fresh start?

Cycles of alcohol abuse affect individuals, families and communities. For each person who tries to break away, there are innumerable pressures forcing them back into familiar patterns. And for those that can't escape, that are fated to make the same choices again and again – can we still feel compassion?

My Epileptic Lurcher

Des Dillon

ISBN 978 1906307 74 5 PBK £7.99

The incredible story of Bailey, the dog who walked on the ceiling; and Manny, the guy who got kicked out of Alcoholics Anonymous for swearing.

Manny is newly married, with a puppy, a flat by the sea, and the BBC on the verge of greenlighting one of his projects. Everything sounds perfect. But Manny has always been an anger management casualty, and the idyllic village life is turning out to be more *League of Gentlemen* than *The Good Life*. As his marriage suffers under the strain of his constant rages, a strange connection begins to emerge between Manny's temper and the health of his beloved lurcher.

... one of the most effortlessly charming books I've read in a long time.

SCOTTISH REVIEW OF BOOKS

Me and Ma Gal

Des Dillon

ISBN 978 1842820 54 4 PBK £5.99

If you never had to get married an that I really think that me an Gal'd be pals for ever. That's not to say that we never fought. Man we had some great fights so we did.

A story of boyhood friendship and irrepressible vitality told with the speed of trains and the understanding of the awkwardness, significance and fragility of that time. This is a day in the life of two boys as told by one of them, 'Derruck Danyul Riley'.

Dillon's book is arguably one of the most frenetic and kinetic, living and breathing of all Scottish novels... The whole novel crackles with this verbal energy.

THE LIST / SCOTTISH BOOK TRUST 100 Best Scottish Books of All Time, 2005

Monks

Des Dillon

ISBN 978 1905222 75 9 PBK £7.99

Three men are off from Coatbridge to an idyllic Italian monastic retreat in search of inner peace and sanctuary.

... like hell they are. Italian food, sunshine and women – it's the perfect holiday in exchange for some easy construction work at the monastery.

Some holiday it turns out to be, what with optional Mass at 5am, a mad monk with a ball and chain, and the salami fiasco – to say nothing of the language barrier.

But even on this remote and tranquil mountain, they can't hide from the chilling story of Jimmy Brogan. Suddenly the past explodes into the present, and they find more redemption than they ever bargained for.

This story... is simultaneously hilarious and touching, morose and vividly energetic, but it is the seamless juxtaposition of the protagonists' internal and external worlds, added to the wonderfully wacky, frenetic narrative, that gives it its fire.
THE HERALD

Picking Brambles

Des Dillon

ISBN 978 1842820 21 6 PBK £6.99

The first pick from over 1,000 poems written by Des Dillon, selected and introduced by Brian Whittingham.

I always considered myself to be first and foremost, a poet. Unfortunately nobody else did. The further away from poetry I moved the more successful I became as a writer. This collection for me is the pinnacle of my writing career. Simply because is my belief that poetry is at the cutting edge of language. Out there breaking new ground in the creation of meaning.

DES DILLON

... to spend an hour in Dillon's company and listen to his quick-fire verbal delivery is to sample the undiluted language of the man that is the raw material used in the crafting of his writing.

BRIAN WHITTINGHAM

Six Black Candles

Des Dillon

ISBN 978 1906307 49 3   PBK   £8.99

'Where's Stacie Gracie's head?' ... sharing space with the sweetcorn and two-for-one lemon meringue pies... in the freezer.

Caroline's husband abandons her (bad move) for Stacie Gracie, his assistant at the meat counter, and incurs more wrath than he anticipated. Caroline, her five sisters, mother and granny, all with a penchant for witchery, invoke the lethal spell of the Six Black Candles. A natural reaction to the break up of a marriage?

Set in present day Irish Catholic Coatbridge, *Six Black Candles* is bound together by the ropes of traditional storytelling and the strength of female familial relationships. Bubbling under the cauldron of superstition, witchcraft and religion is the heat of revenge; and the love and venom of sisterhood.

The writing is always truthful, immediate and powerful.

SCOTLAND ON SUNDAY

The Glasgow Dragon

Des Dillon

ISBN 978 1842820 56 8 PBK £9.99

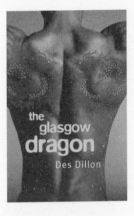

What do I want? Let me see now. I want to destroy you spiritually, emotionally and mentally before I destroy you physically.

When Christie Devlin goes into business with a triad to take control of the Glasgow drug market, little does he know that his downfall and the destruction of his family is being plotted. As Devlin struggles with his own demons the real fight is just beginning.

There are some things you should never forgive yourself for.

Nothing is as simple as good and evil. Des Dillon is a master storyteller and this is a world he knows well.

Des Dillon writes like a man possessed. The words come tumbling out of him. ... His prose... teems with unceasing energy.
THE SCOTSMAN

Details of these and other books published by Luath Press can be found at:

www.luath.co.uk

Luath Press Limited

committed to publishing well written books worth reading

LUATH PRESS takes its name from Robert Burns, whose little collie Luath (*Gael.*, swift or nimble) tripped up Jean Armour at a wedding and gave him the chance to speak to the woman who was to be his wife and the abiding love of his life. Burns called one of 'The Twa Dogs' Luath after Cuchullin's hunting dog in Ossian's *Fingal*. Luath Press was established in 1981 in the heart of Burns country, and now resides a few steps up the road from Burns' first lodgings on Edinburgh's Royal Mile.

Luath offers you distinctive writing with a hint of unexpected pleasures.

Most bookshops in the UK, the US, Canada, Australia, New Zealand and parts of Europe either carry our books in stock or can order them for you. To order direct from us, please send a £sterling cheque, postal order, international money order or your credit card details (number, address of cardholder and expiry date) to us at the address below. Please add post and packing as follows: UK – £1.00 per delivery address; overseas surface mail – £2.50 per delivery address; overseas airmail – £3.50 for the first book to each delivery address, plus £1.00 for each additional book by airmail to the same address. If your order is a gift, we will happily enclose your card or message at no extra charge.

Luath Press Limited
543/2 Castlehill
The Royal Mile
Edinburgh EH1 2ND
Scotland

Telephone: 0131 225 4326 (24 hours)
Fax: 0131 225 4324
Email: sales@luath.co.uk
Website: www.luath.co.uk